Weather Watch

Rain

Honor Head

QEB Publishing, Inc.

Copyright © QEB Publishing, Inc. 2006

First published in the United States by
QEB Publishing, Inc.
23062 La Cadena Drive
Laguna Hills, CA 92653
www.qeb-publishing.com

Library of Congress Control Number: 2005911006

ISBN 978-1-59566-229-3

Written by Honor Head
Designed by Melissa Alaverdy
Consultant Terry Jennings
Editor Hannah Ray
Picture Researcher Joanne Forrest Smith
Illustrations Chris Davidson
Diagrams Jonathan Vipond

Publisher Steve Evans
Editorial Director Jean Coppendale
Art Director Zeta Davies

Printed and bound in China

Picture credits

Words in **bold** can be found in the glossary on page 22.

Contents

Rain

When it rains, everything gets wet.

You can keep dry in the rain by wearing a waterproof coat and rubber boots, and putting up an umbrella.

After a shower or heavy rainfall, big puddles appear.

If you are wearing rubber boots, or **galoshes**,
it is fun to splash through puddles.

There are many different types of rain. Drizzle is
a light rain. However, during a thunderstorm there
can be very heavy rain. Sometimes it can rain all day,
but a shower can last for just a few minutes.

Why do we need rain?

Rain is very important for all living things.

Without rain, we wouldn't have rivers, streams, lakes, or ponds. There would be nowhere for fish and water birds to live. Wild animals would have nothing to drink.

Many different types of birds live by lakes and rivers. Some birds, such as this swan, build their nests on water.

The water we use for drinking, washing, and cooking comes from lakes and rivers that were filled by rain. Rain also helps to keep our streets clean and our fields, trees, and gardens green.

Before we can drink rainwater, it has to be specially cleaned.

Why does it rain?

Rain comes from clouds in the sky.
A cloud is a **mass** of water droplets.

1. The sun shines on water, making it warm. The water turns into an invisible gas called **water vapor**.

2. The water vapor rises into the air, where it cools down. When the water vapor cools, it forms clouds of water droplets.

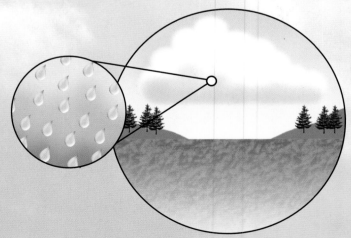

Airplanes and birds can travel through clouds. It is like moving through fog.

3. The droplets join together until they are the size of raindrops.

4. When they are heavy enough, the water droplets fall back to Earth as rain.

Thunderstorms

Thunder, lightning, and heavy rain happen during thunderstorms.

Thunderclouds build up when it is hot outdoors and water droplets rise very high into the air. The water droplets freeze and become tiny bits of ice which bump into each other. This causes **lightning**, which is a flash of electricity.

If there is lightning, you will usually hear thunder. This is a loud rumble or boom in the sky that happens after the lightning strikes.

Sometimes lightning comes out of the cloud and down to the Earth.

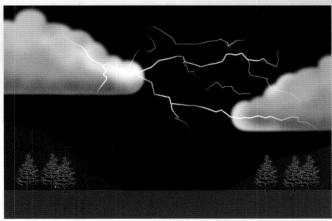

At other times, lightning moves between two clouds.

Too much rain

Heavy rain can sometimes cause floods.

Floods usually happen in places that are close to water, such as a river. The rain can make rivers overflow. Water rushes onto the land and can cause a lot of damage.

Some hot countries, such as India, have a time of the year when it rains almost nonstop for many weeks. This is called a **monsoon**.

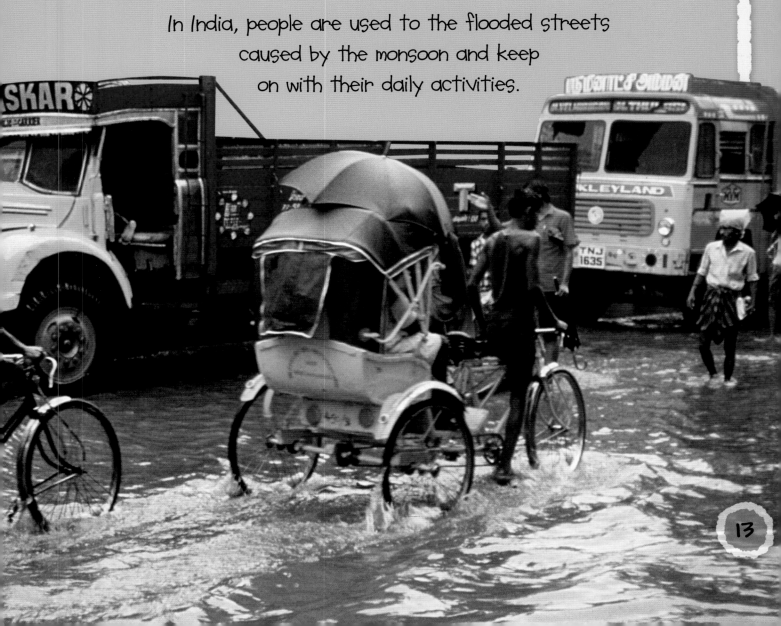

In India, people are used to the flooded streets caused by the monsoon and keep on with their daily activities.

Not enough rain

In some parts of the world, it doesn't rain for months and months.

If it doesn't rain, and it is also very hot, a country may have a **drought**. This means there is not enough water for everyone to use.

Some very hot countries have droughts that last for a year or more. This means that the people cannot grow enough food and they might **starve**.

If there is no rain, forests and fields become very dry. A single spark can start fires that burn for weeks. These fires cause a lot of damage.

Rain and plants

Trees, flowers, and other plants need rain and sun to grow.

When the soil is warm and it rains, plants start to grow.

When it is very hot, flowers in the garden need to be watered every day or they will die.

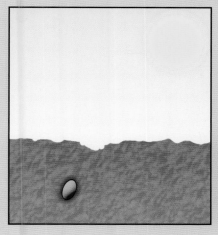

seed in the soil

rain and sun

shoot from the seed grows toward the sun

In a rainforest, it is hot and wet all the time. Trees grow high into the sky and the ground is covered in plants.

In a rainforest, plants grow very quickly because it rains every day.

Rainbows

Sometimes, when it is raining,
a rainbow appears in the sky. This
happens when the sun shines
through the raindrops.

You will only see a rainbow when it is raining and the sun is shining.

The rainbow is made up of seven colors. The colors always appear in the same order: red, orange, yellow, green, blue, indigo, and violet. Some people say you should make a wish when you see a rainbow.

Rainy-day activities

Here are some fun things to do if it is raining outside.

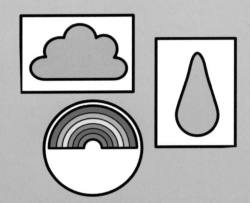

Make a rain mobile

1. Using pieces of construction paper or paper plates, draw and color some huge raindrops, some clouds, and a rainbow. Make sure they are all about the same size.

2. Ask an adult to help you to cut out your pictures and make a hole at the top of each one.

3. Thread some string or thin ribbon through the holes and tie each one to a clothes hanger.

Eat a rainbow

You will need an adult to help you with this activity.

1. Ask an adult to bake or buy a round sponge cake. Get some frosting and a selection of food colorings in different rainbow colors.

2. With an adult's help, make up some red frosting and, using a piping bag with a round tip, draw a circle around the outside of the top of the cake.

3. Make up some orange frosting and draw a circle inside the red circle.

4. Add other frosting circles, one inside the other, in the remaining colors of the rainbow.

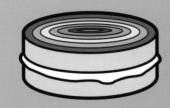

5. Cut the cake in half and you have two rainbow cakes.

Glossary

drought   a long period of dry weather

galoshes   waterproof boots, worn over your usual shoes

lightning   electricity that builds up in clouds and is seen as a flash of light

mass   a large group of something

monsoon   the name given to the rains that fall for many weeks, or even months, in some hot countries

starve   when people do not have enough to eat and they die

water vapor   an invisible gas that rises into the air from water when it is warmed

Index

Parents' and teachers' notes

- Look at the cover of the book. Discuss the title and the picture. What do the children think the book is about? What are they expecting to see inside? Are the children looking forward to reading the book?

- Look at the pictures inside. Explain the difference between diagrams and photographs. Explain the function of the captions.

- When you have read the book, ask the children what they liked best about it.

- Ask the children to talk about what they associate with rain, for example, being stuck inside, having fun playing in puddles, using umbrellas, wearing rubber boots and waterproof coats.

- Discuss why rain is good (for example, it provides us with water to drink) and when rain can be bad (for example, when it causes floods).

- Count how many glasses of water each child drinks a day. Soft drinks are mostly water and so is fruit juice, so include these, too. Remember that all of these were once rain!

- Ask the children to draw a picture of a thunderstorm and a picture of a gentle shower. Put the artworks on the wall next to each other. Discuss the differences in the pictures, such as the color of the sky, etc.

- Ask the children to write a story involving rain.

- Design an umbrella. Ask the children to draw the outline of an umbrella. Encourage them to decorate their umbrellas in any colors and patterns they want. Put the pictures on the wall to create a colorful display.

- Discuss thunderstorms. Are there any children who are scared of thunder and lightning? Why?

PLEASE NOTE
- The activity on page 21 is not suitable for children with an intolerance to food colorings.